(C) LegendaryLifeMedia.∆

Legal Notice

This book is only for personal use. You cannot amend, distribute, sell, use, quote or paraphrase any part, or the content within this book, without the consent of the publisher.

Table of Contents

Welcome to the practice of Journaling!

It's safe to assume if you are reading this workbook, then you are ready to begin to keep a personal journal.

The information you are about to read will take you one step closer to a life of fulfilling journaling.

Instead of tips and encouragement, you'll learn direct steps that will help you commit to the art of journaling.

If you are ready to find out just how personally powerful journaling can be, please read on!

One of the most powerful self-care steps you can take is to embrace the art of journaling. You might feel like dismissing this, but before you do, take a look at a few facts.

Studies have shown:

- People who journal experience better moods.
- Journaling helps to reduce stress.
- Regular journaling is an effective tool to fight depression and anxiety.
- People who journal don't get sick as often.
- Journaling can even help people to fight common diseases.
- Healing from medical procedures occurs faster in people who journal as opposed to those who don't.

Wow, seems very powerful doesn't it?

The good news is there is no one-size-fits-all kind of journaling you must do in order to reap those benefits. You can journal in a variety of ways depending on your likes and needs.

In the following pages we will explore those components a little closer. Read on to learn about the power of Journaling.

NOTE: In this book you will come across prompts to do some basic journaling. These journal prompts are designed to get you used to the concept of journaling.

Don't worry about grammar or content. There's no wrong way to do this, though, for maximum benefit, it's recommended to write things out by hand physically.

This is freeform writing, without planning, so relax as you jot down these first thoughts.

The Power of Journaling

In terms of self-help, there are few things quite so effective at changing your life as journaling.

In fact, journaling is one of those 'keystone' habits, as talked about by Charles Duhigg, in his book, *The Power of Habit*. He describes how keystone habits tend to build a whole host of other positive habits around them almost entirely by themselves.

Think of how a decluttering habit leads to cleaner and tidier surroundings at home, eventually affecting your workspace. The decluttering habit may then move into non-tangible areas of your life, such as your relationships.

That's because a keystone habit is found at the core of other patterns. In the decluttering example, the core concept is to remove things from your life you no longer need, or no longer give you joy. This will force you to examine the objects you have in your life.

As you get used to journaling, you start noticing other areas of life where you're holding onto things you no longer need, and that don't give you joy. This very naturally leads to things like the 'decluttering' of relationships, or the sudden desire for a shift in career.

Now think of journaling as a keystone habit. What is at the core of journaling which makes it so significant?

The core of journaling is not only the ability to express yourself but the *need* to.

Journaling forces you to examine and understand the world around you. At the same time, it places you within the world, inviting you to see and understand your role in things.

This constant examination and re-examination of yourself is a powerful thing with far-reaching consequences.

The Obvious Benefits

Even if you never reach beyond the surface of journaling, you will still find numerous positive benefits.

Let's look at those first:

You Experience Personal Expression
Being able to put into words how you perceive the world is a feeling like no other. The very act of doing so gives a sense of great satisfaction. After all, these are your impressions, put forth uniquely in your own voice.

You Give off Creative Sparks
The more you write, the more you'll see how things fit together. This leads to new ideas starting with a "what if..." and goes from there into creative leaps, taking you into fresh and new territory waiting to be explored.

You Cement Learning
Even the things you already know become more concrete and tangible once you set them down on paper. If you really want to understand something thoroughly, journal about it.

You Put Things in Order
Writing things down helps you easily see what you need to do and how to go about doing it. This is organization, plain and simple. It enables you to accomplish more while feeling less frazzled.

You Realize Goals
When you journal, you set down your visions and dreams for the future and, at the same time, create the roadmap to get you there.

Writing about goals on a regular basis keeps you inspired. Writing about the steps along the way helps you keep on course to reach those goals. It's so helpful to track your progress and mark down each milestone as you reach it.

You Become a Historian

Your journal becomes a record of your personal history. No one else is experiencing the world in the same way you are. Your impressions, the very actions of your life have importance. Because you journal, you preserve what it means to be you, here in this moment for your future self—and even generations to come.

You Become a Writer

In the end, the daily act of writing develops your ability with words; a habit of putting thoughts on paper and a voice uniquely your own. You have become a writer, ready to stretch your wings and fly into the world of stories, articles, and books if you so desire.

Where the Magic Really Happens

What you may not realize is journaling takes you much deeper into a world you might not even be aware of.

The true power of journaling is how it affects you personally, in your interactions with others, and your understanding of yourself.

Your Mood Improves

When you write things freely, you're given the ability to vent on paper. This action has a way of removing the dreck of the day from you; you immediately start feeling better.

Your Anxiety / Depression Disappears

While journaling might not be the cure for a panic attack just yet, the very act of writing about the things causing worry and angst helps put things into perspective.

At the very least, journaling traps them on paper and removes them from your mind so you can better process these worries.

This step-back is what enables you to take a deep breath and relax so you don't get so caught up in a worry/depression spiral where you can't see the forest for the trees.

You Gain Clarity

If you're having trouble figuring out the best course of action with a problem, writing about it is a sure way to get a clearer perspective.

Many times, we're simply too close to the situation. When you step back and try to put things into words, generally you start seeing things you may have missed, and as a result, gain better insight to your next steps.

You See Things as They Are

We are not always as honest with ourselves as we would like to be.

Journaling is what forces us to see the lies we tell ourselves so that we can see past them to the truth. Thankfully, the act of journaling, while calling us on our BS, is also non-judgmental. This isn't something we can always say about our friends!

You Become a Problem-Solver

The very act of writing down a problem often leads directly to a solution.

If not, the writing process becomes a way to work through the options to solve whatever problem is plaguing you. This gets interesting when used as a process because you're triggering the creative side of the brain over the logic side when you use writing. This enables you to find solutions you might not otherwise.

Helps You to See the Rhythm of Your Life

Nothing helps you to get a better handle on the routines, habits, and cycles of your daily life than writing down your actions every day.

After a while of doing this kind of writing, you start to see where the patterns are, good and bad. This enables you to address habits and poor choices with an eye toward change.

Journaling Becomes Therapy

Only writing allows you to work through complicated emotions so thoroughly. By journaling about the peaks and valleys, and then working to determine what causes moods and triggers, journaling helps you identify better courses of actions. This is why journaling is such a favorite tool of therapists, making it a part of your daily recovery process.

You Get to Know Yourself Better

The more you work through the deeper issues, the more you start to understand your own moods and reasons for doing things. This kind of self-knowledge is a great thing to possess.

You Start to Understand Forgiveness

When you write about the things that hurt you in the past, you also learn how to let those things go.

This is how you finally move beyond the past and come to embrace the future. A necessary step here is forgiveness. Journaling is the perfect place to work out those complex emotions of hurt and betrayal so you can finally lay them to rest.

If there are relationships you need to be healed from in order for this to happen, you have the place to work through the emotions holding you back from being able to do so.

You Deal with the Past

Sometimes the act of laying things to rest isn't quite so easy as forgiveness and moving on.

Some hurts take time to work through, especially those that happened in childhood when you didn't have the understanding of what was truly going on.

Journaling helps you to work through those memories, giving you clarity and understanding you can use moving forward. You might have to do some work here, to rewire the messages your past is trying to provide you with.

Luckily, journaling is an excellent tool for working through damaging messages from the past and turning them into more positive statements of self-affirmation.

You Change in your Treatment of Others

Have you ever had trouble putting yourself in someone else's shoes?

It might be easier to try it in writing first. Discover true empathy as you become more sensitive to those around you. Journaling teaches compassion.

You Resolve Disagreements Better

Empathy might put you in someone else's shoes, but it can't make them like you.

When you have a disagreement, where do you turn? Your journal can help you work through the details of what went wrong. It also gives you a place to rehearse the dialogue necessary to resolve the disagreement. When the time comes, you will have the words needed to act as a peacemaker.

You Discover Truth About Yourself

Journaling reveals a lot more than your basic likes and dislikes.

As you write, you're going to discover a lot of truths about yourself, even some that have remained hidden until now. You learn what drives your emotions as well as your actions. This knowledge can help enable you to work through your negative behavior patterns.

The beauty of this is how much stronger you come away after the fact. You start to see all the ways you're connected with the rest of the world and your importance in those connections. You come to trust the person you're becoming, and even to like yourself. In short, journaling helps you to become your very best version of you.

It Puts you in Balance with the World

There is a certain harmony that comes from living a life in tune with the world.

Journaling helps you to see where you fit in. You find connections to the world around you, to the people and things in your life. You discover the symbiotic nature of life and come to embrace your part in the universe. In this aspect of things, journaling truly does inspire peace and unity.

Journaling and Your Physical Health

Journaling has proven time and again to help fight stress. Stress if one of the worst things for our health. It affects our diet, sleep and mood. On top of that, it releases damaging hormones into our body.

Reducing stress is often the trigger to a whole host of health benefits. As a stress relief tool, journaling can actually boost your physical health.

If you remember the list from the introduction, we already pointed out that people who journal:

- Have a better immune system
- Tend to do better in medical treatment
- Heal more quickly in a post-operative environment

Why? It all goes back to the stress component.

The very act of writing about things you are connected to emotionally activates certain areas in your brain. When these areas are activated, you can generate a more pleasurable mood and function cognitively at a higher level. All of which helps you come up with creative solutions to any potential problems or stressors in your life.

In short, journaling gives some of the benefits you'd get if you were ranting to your best friend!

Journaling also gives you the added bonus of an increase in reasoning skills and a shift in mood that is more long-lasting than what you would get in a rant session with your BFF.

People who are less stressed have better immune systems, heal faster, and tend to enjoy a better quality of life.

Nowhere is this more evident than in people who are going through serious medical issues.

Journaling has been proven to raise the quality of life in patients. Those who journal while dealing with a severe medical condition do better in accepting their diagnosis, and also in processing everything that goes along with it. These patients do far better in treatment than those who do not journal.

In the end, it's impossible to deny the benefits that come from journaling. With so many reasons to journal, the only question remaining at this point is how to go about getting started.

Which one of these journaling benefits appeals to you the most? Why?

There is a Journal for Everything

Once you've decided to journal, you only need to find a blank book of some kind to jot things down in, right?

For most people, it's not quite so easy. Nothing inspires writer's block faster than a blank page. To combat this feeling of imminent failure, the simplest solution is the most obvious one: Decide what you want to write about before you even begin.

Easy, right?

While this might work for a journal entry or two, the truth is most people do best by using a themed journal, especially when just starting.

By picking out only one kind of thing to write about, you put yourself into a particular mindset daily. You'll even find yourself looking for things that match your theme as you go about your daily life.

For example, if you want to start a gratitude journal, you will find yourself developing a habit of looking for things you're grateful throughout the day so that you can include them in your daily journal.

This brings us to the added benefit of themed journals: They do make an impact into your day to day living.

What are some examples of themed journals?

Gratitude Journal

The Gratitude Journal is just what you think it would be. You only write about the things you're grateful for every day.

While this seems straightforward, especially for those who like making bullet lists, it's not always. The idea is to build a positive mindset. In order to reach this goal most effectively, you need to avoid repetition.

The good news is there's plenty to be grateful about in your day to day life. It could be as simple as you are being grateful for getting a great parking spot or happy you get to enjoy a sunny day.

You don't need to find great big things to fill the pages. Writing in a gratitude journal will help you start seeing all the simple things in life to be appreciated for too.

For maximum impact, write down three items you're thankful for every day.

Success Journal

A Success Journal has a different tone altogether.

While there will be plenty of gratitude in its pages, for this journal you should focus on simply recording some of your wins and successes along the way.

This might not even be a journal you keep every single day. This is the type of journal you break out when needed. The whole idea here is to compile a list of encouraging moments and motivating wins.

Any time you have a "win" in life, jot it down in your journal. You can spend some time explaining why it was important to you as well.

This way, the next time you are feeling down, or ready to give up – you can read the journal. You will have a list of "receipts" right in front of you that proves you have succeeded in the past – so you can do it again!

A friend of mine is an entrepreneur. She keeps a journal of all the nice comments she gets from her clients. This way, when she gets some bad feedback, or is feeling like a failure, she can read her journal. This reminds her of all of the people she has helped and made happy. What is more motivating than that?

Goal Journal

The focus here is on creating a very specific goal and following this goal to completion. This journal keeps track of the steps along the way.

Your goal journal is a recording of your failures as well as your successes. More importantly it includes what you learn from both.

Some people think of their Goal Journal as a business document as though it's an accountability log for your business or job.

We encourage you to take it far beyond a mere recitation of facts. Use your Goal Journal to note how you feel about the goal or to explore the fears or difficulties that might be holding you back from realizing your goal.

You can make the Goal Journal as personal as you want.

To begin, define the goal you want to attain, making it as concrete as possible. Lay out your roadmap for how you intend to get there. Add deadlines for accountability.

Most importantly though - start taking action!

Habit Journal

A Habit Journal does just what it sounds like – it helps you to form new habits.

Considering how long it takes to build a habit, the point here is to keep track of your progress in developing new behaviors into your life.

More than a calendar where you might mark down whether you performed that habit on this particular day, a Habit Journal expects you to be accountable at the end of the day. You begin by listing the habits you wish to form, following up by scheduling those habits (here's where you might want to use a calendar or an app on your phone to give you periodic reminders of the pattern).

At the end of each day, you want to spend a few minutes journaling about your habit experience.

Remember, this is a journal, so you're not just writing down whether or not you performed the habit, but what happened when you did.

- How did it feel?
- Were there roadblocks along the way?
- Was there something unexpected that cropped up, such as a trigger you maybe need to work through?

Sometimes what blocks us from accomplishing a goal, such as a new habit, is something from the past. Your Habit Journal is the perfect place to work through those thoughts and emotions.

Begin by making a list of new habits you'd like to add to your daily routine. Choose only one or two to work on at a time, so you don't burn yourself out.

Food Journal

A Food Journal is pretty straightforward.

In it, you track what you eat with an eye toward healthy nutrition and ultimately improved health.

Generally, this is used for weight management. But you can use a Food Journal to track foods for other reasons, such as keeping track of the sugars in the foods you eat if you have diabetes.

This kind of journal is more important than you probably think. It's been proven in countless studies that people who kept a food journal met their weight loss goals, or other health-related goals, more frequently than those who did not. Don't get too caught up in just listing foods though.

Your Food Journal should also be a place to explore your feelings toward food, especially if you find you're an emotional eater.

Begin by stating your goals for your journal and by expressing your feelings about food in general. After that, dive right into recording the foods you eat, not forgetting to chart your progress as you go.

Health Journal

The Health Journal goes beyond the Food Journal as it chronicles more than just what you eat.

In a Health Journal, you might monitor things like pain levels, attacks on your health such as seizures or flare-ups, or things like diet, exercise, and sleep.

You use a Health Journal to look for patterns, to ascertain triggers and food allergies, or to measure your efforts to improve your health overall.

Like the Habit Journal or the Goal Journal, you might want to pursue new behaviors and practices. But in a Health Journal, you also include the details about how you feel and what your body is doing.

The best way to start this journal is with an assessment of your current health, and some concrete goals on how you would like to improve it.

Bullet Journal

A Bullet Journal is not so much a theme as a style, but it works particularly well if you're one of those people who enjoy making lists.

It's exactly what it sounds like—a place to write things down in a list format rather than in long rambling posts.

A Bullet Journal can be used in any context, such as gratitude, tracking goals and monitoring your progress in life.

For those of an artistic bent, there's a surprising amount of room for creativity with a Bullet Journal. People often create beautiful looking bullet journals that help appease both their logical and creative mindsets

The nice thing: You can track your whole life in bullet points over a set series of lists, divided into daily goals, monthly goals, and future goals.

Bullet Journaling doesn't take much time out of your day, and because you can keep track of your life at a glance, it's ideal for just about anybody.

Not Every Journal Needs a Theme

Not every type of journal is listed here.

You might decide you want to create a dream journal or a way to track story ideas if you're a writer. Maybe your journal is heavier on artwork than words.

You might just want a simple, non-themed journal. Sometimes this is the most powerful type. You just want to jot down random thoughts each day.

The point is, any kind of journal is fine, so long as it serves _your_ purpose.

Going back to the benefit that you chose in the last chapter, think about the kind of journal you would need to gain this benefit. Write about why you chose this kind of journal. Express how you would like to use this book in the weeks and months to come.

_____

_____

_____

_____

_____

_____

_____

_____

_____

_____

_____

_____

_____

_____

_____

_____

_____

_____

_____

_____

Journaling How-tos

While there is no wrong way to journal so long as you write consistently, there are things you can do to create the maximum amount of impact upon your life.

Write by Hand
Time and again, studies have shown writing out your journal longhand is more beneficial.

Why?

When you write things out by hand, you have better long-term memory recall, meaning you process what you're writing more effectively. This is important when journaling as the whole point of putting things down is to guide you through processing data, whether you're writing details about your day or recalling something that happened years ago.

Another study showed how people who journaled longhand processed the traumatic events they'd experienced much more quickly and were able to move on faster than those who wrote similar entries on a computer.

While there was still measurable benefit for people who wrote on the computer, there was such a significant rate of increase in writing by hand the recommendation was clear: Journaling by hand wins ...er... hands down.

Start Simply
There's no need to go for long, elaborate posts from the get-go.

Write what's comfortable in the format you're most comfortable with. Don't be afraid to switch things up and try new things until you find the model that works best for you.

It's too easy to overwhelm yourself if you get wrapped up in complexities, like having the perfect bullet journal or requiring you to start with an inspirational quote at the top of your entry every day. You can always add in the finer points later as you get more used to the idea of writing every day and feel surer of yourself.

Ignore the Word Count
There is no perfect length for a journal entry.

Write what's on your heart. This might mean three pages of dense text one day, or a bullet-point list another. That's fine. This is *your* journal. You do what you need to do with it.

Embrace Inspiration
If you find yourself with an idea or something you want to write about during the day, make a quick note of it.

Don't lose out on something worth exploring just because it's not your 'regular journaling time.' This spontaneous list will become an essential part of your journal, as it will give you a wealth of ideas to write about when the time comes.

Choose a Time of Day Optimal for Your Needs
Some people swear by journaling in the morning as a way to set up your day on a positive note geared for success. Others like to journal before bed as a way to process the day. Whichever works for you, go with it. While both times of day are loaded with benefits, one is no more 'correct' than the other.

Go into Detail
When writing about an incident, be sure to layer in the details, thereby making the story so much more profound and interesting. These are the words that will bring the memory into sharp focus years later when you re-read the entry.

Focus on the Emotion
When detailing something from your day, try to put an emotion on the incident.

How did you feel at the time? How do you feel now in recalling it? A careful examination of your feelings helps you to process the incident, allowing you to move past it.

Don't Beat Yourself Up

Life happens.

While you do get the most benefit from writing regularly, it might be your schedule doesn't allow for daily journaling. If you write every day and miss a few entries due to being sick or some other life event getting in the way, it's okay.

You're never 'behind' nor do you need to 'make up' for lost entries by writing extras. Simply pick up where you left off next time and go from there.

Make Journaling Part of Your Routine

If you strive to make journaling part of your routine – you will be less likely to forget or skip it.

When you figure out what time works best for you, try to stay consistent with that.

Even better, connect your journaling routine with an existing pattern in your life. If you have a morning or bed-time routine, try to fit journaling in with it. When you do this, journaling can become as second nature as brushing your teeth.

Forget Perfectionism
Mistakes happen.

You spell something wrong when using ink or create a mess. You cross things out as you reconsider what you've said. You get distracted and doodle all over the page.

Who cares?

It's all part of the process. A journal is a reflection of you at the moment. Embrace who you are, random artwork and all. Write from the heart. Content matters, not how it's presented on the page.

Get Artistic
If you want to play with design and graphics, create a Bullet Journal. Or if you're into art, consider a Self-portrait Journal where you try to express who you are in by drawing yourself each day.

Add artwork, cartoons, or creativity to every corner of the page. Decorate with flowers or skulls. Draw whatever suits your mood! Journaling doesn't have to be about just the words on the page.

Try a Brain Dump
Feeling muddled, with too much going on at once? Throw it all on the page in a glorious stream of writing to clear it out of your head. Sometimes you need to let go of everything you've been holding in.

Let Therapy Happen
You might not have realized just how deep you might go while journaling.

One minute you're writing about your cat, the next you're lost in some childhood trauma you'd all but forgotten.

When this happens, write what comes to you. Allow yourself to work through the memory and explore why it's coming up now. At the same time, remind yourself this incident happened in the past. Try to let it go when you're done writing.

Which one of these tips do you struggle with or resist the most? Which speaks to you? Write about the one that stands out and explore why it does.

Commit Yourself, but start slowly

If you want to commit to journaling, you are going to need some motivation. That might seem potentially overwhelming, but all we are looking for here is the "why".

Once you know the why then you can start working on the how.

Take some time now to fill out the following three prompts:

Why Are You Considering Journaling Now?

What Do You Plan on Journaling About?

List the Ways You Think Journaling can Help You.

Use a Writing Prompt

This section is all about getting started.

Journal prompts are a great way to get the creative juices flowing.

As you read the prompts, feel free to adapt and change them as they give you the seed of an idea.

Go wherever the ideas take you!

To begin, we will share 7 journal prompts, one for each day of the following week as an exercise in journaling.

You simply follow the prompt and write! If you can commit to this for a week, you can commit to this for months, or even years. We provide one page for you to write, but don't think you have to fill it completely.

Let's begin!

Day One

If you could change one thing about yourself what would it be?
How would your life look?
What's stopping you from changing this thing?

Day Two

What is your all-time favorite quote?
Why is it your favorite quote?
What meaning does it have in your current life?

Day Three

Think about someone you really miss. It could be someone who passed away, or as simple as someone you haven't seen in a while. What would you say to this person?

Day Four

What scares you the most? What is your biggest fear? Does it hold you back in life, if so – why?

Day Five

Look at your last few hours of texts, choose one and turn it into a short story. Don't worry about too much about the length.

Day Six

You wake up and realize you are a billionaire.
How did you make the money?

Day Seven

You are lying in bed and just about to fall asleep. As you are about to drift off, the phone rings. Describe that call.

Use a Writing Prompt, Continued

Congratulations on finishing your first week of journaling!

How did it go? Was it as hard as you thought it might be? Or did you find out wishing you had more space to write in?

Regardless, you've come a long way in the art of journaling!

Now, we share 30 more prompts for you to fill in as a continued exercise. You'll have one page for each prompt, but again, don't think you have to fill every page.

What are you looking forward to today?

If you were moving across the country and could only take a limited number of objects, what would you choose no matter what, and why?

Imagine yourself as a bird or animal.
What have you chosen?
What do you think it would feel like to be this animal?

What is your earliest memory?
Write it in as much detail as possible.

What is your body trying to tell you that you haven't been listening to? How would you like to reply?

Write about a time you helped someone. How do you think this act made them feel? How did you feel performing it?

Who are the three most influential people in your life? How have they impacted you?

Write 12 things you'd like to do over the next year, listing one for each month.

Talk about the first time you did something you never had before, particularly one you felt like everyone knew how to do but you. How did you feel when you accomplished this task?

Who hurt your feelings in the past? Write about why they might have acted in the way they did. Does active empathy change your how you feel about the situation?

What has surprised you?

What is something you believed as a child that you found out wasn't true as an adult?

If you had the ability to teleport yourself anywhere, where would you go?

Who is someone you used to talk to a lot, but haven't in a while?
How would you go about reconnecting with them?
What would you want to say?

If you could leave a message to the you of last year, what would you say?

What is your perfect day?

Write about something you wished you had said to someone but never did. Say it to them now in the safety of your journal.

What is something you'd like to learn?

What secret do you wish you could tell someone? What do you think would happen if you did? Seriously consider sharing this secret with someone close, so you no longer need to carry it.

List off your five favorite meals.
Make plans to enjoy one of them shortly.

What are the five things you like about yourself?

You've been given a thousand dollars and an hour to spend it, the rules being it has to be for something fun. What would you do?

How can you show kindness to someone today (if you're journaling in the morning) or tomorrow (if you're journaling at night)? Make plans to do so.

What do you dream about doing more than anything else in the world? Write about it in detail.

What is the last book or movie that made an impact on you?
What about it made it unforgettable?

Pick a color (it doesn't have to be your favorite). Tell how this color makes you feel inside.

You're lost in a foreign country where you don't speak the language. Is this a crisis, a challenge, or an opportunity? Why?

List six things you've learned recently that you found fascinating.

Describe your favorite time of day. What memory do you associate with this time of day that makes it your favorite?

Ellen Sirleaf Johnson said, "If your dreams do not scare you, they are not big enough." What is the dream that scares you? What can you do that will set you on the path to achieving this dream?

Welcome to the world of Journaling!

Now that you've started, the only thing left is to continue!

It might not feel like it, but if you spent the past week and then some following the prompts, then you are officially keeping a journal.

How did it make you feel? Do you see any benefits yet?

No matter the answers to the above, commit to continue on.

It's too early in the journey to quit yet. Just take things one week at a time.

Eventually you will know exactly how powerful a tool journaling can be.

The rest of this book will allow you to continue what you started during the last week, unprompted!

Don't feel rushed; don't feel pressured. Work at your own pace with the mindset to write in this journal on a regular basis.

Best wishes, and let your thoughts flow from your mind to your pen!

Today's Date: _____ *Today's Thoughts:*

Today's Date: _____ *Today's Thoughts:*

Today's Date:

Today's Thoughts:

Today's Date: _____   *Today's Thoughts:*

_____

_____

_____

_____

_____

_____

_____

_____

_____

_____

_____

_____

_____

_____

_____

_____

_____

_____

_____

Today's Date: _____ _Today's Thoughts:_

Today's Date: _____ *Today's Thoughts:*

Today's Date: _____ *Today's Thoughts:*

Today's Date: _____   *Today's Thoughts:*

Today's Date: _____ *Today's Thoughts:*

Today's Date: _____ *Today's Thoughts:*

Today's Date: _____ *Today's Thoughts:*

Today's Date: _____ *Today's Thoughts:*

Today's Date: _____ *Today's Thoughts:*

100

Today's Date: _____ *Today's Thoughts:*

Today's Date: *Today's Thoughts:*

Today's Date: *Today's Thoughts:*

Today's Date: *Today's Thoughts:*

Today's Date: _____ *Today's Thoughts:*

Today's Date: _____ *Today's Thoughts:*

_____
_____
_____
_____
_____
_____
_____
_____
_____
_____
_____
_____
_____
_____
_____
_____
_____
_____
_____
_____
_____
_____
_____

Today's Date: *Today's Thoughts:*

Today's Date: _____   ## Today's Thoughts:

Today's Date: _____ *Today's Thoughts:*

Today's Date: _____   *Today's Thoughts:*

Today's Date: _Today's Thoughts:_

Today's Date: *Today's Thoughts:*

Today's Thoughts:

Today's Date: _____ *Today's Thoughts:*

_____

_____

_____

_____

_____

_____

_____

_____

_____

_____

_____

_____

_____

_____

_____

_____

_____

_____

_____

_____

_____

Today's Date: _____   *Today's Thoughts:*

Today's Date: _____ *Today's Thoughts:*

Today's Date: _____ *Today's Thoughts:*

Today's Date: _____   *Today's Thoughts:*

_____

_____

_____

_____

_____

_____

_____

_____

_____

_____

_____

_____

_____

_____

_____

_____

_____

_____

_____

_____

Today's Date: _____   *Today's Thoughts:*

Today's Date: _____ Today's Thoughts:

Today's Date: *Today's Thoughts:*

Today's Date: *Today's Thoughts:*

Today's Date: *Today's Thoughts:*

Today's Date: _____ _Today's Thoughts:_

Today's Date: _Today's Thoughts:_

Today's Date: _____ *Today's Thoughts:*

143

Today's Date: *Today's Thoughts:*

Today's Date: _____ *Today's Thoughts:*

Today's Date: _____ Today's Thoughts:

Today's Date: _____ *Today's Thoughts:*

_____

_____

_____

_____

_____

_____

_____

_____

_____

_____

_____

_____

_____

_____

_____

_____

_____

_____

_____

_____

_____

More From LegendaryLifeMedia.net

Living a legendary life, essentially, means that you're living your best life. It means trying to maximize the potential in everything you do to give yourself the best chance of feeling good. It means achieving more and experiencing maximum happiness. It means that you exploit your potential to the full and seize opportunities whenever they present themselves. It also means you pursue your dreams freely without allowing yourself to be held back from achieving everything you could.

To start living a legendary life, visit **WiredForALegendaryLife.com**. We'll give you practical tips to help you achieve your full potential. Discover how you can implement change to make your life the best it can be.

For more information on our books, scan the QR code below.

Made in the USA
Monee, IL
28 November 2023

47592395R00087